ESTATE PLANNING FOR SINGLE MOTHERS

A comprehensive guide to protecting your children's future.

SHERLEY FLORIVAL

*"Children are not born for the benefit of their parents,
neither are they the property of their family.
Children belong to the future."*

Anthon St. Maarten

Published in the United States by Absolute Author Publishing House
www.absoluteauthorpublishinghouse.com

Absolute Author
Publishing House

Paperback ISBN: 9781649537560
E-Book ISBN: 9781649537577

Editor: Sherley Florival

Author: Sherley Florival
www.sherleyflorival.com

To my mother La Reine,
my father Pierre Joseph,
and my son Adonai.

DEDICATION

To all single mothers who wishes to bridge the wealth gap by leaving an inheritance in the form of assets to their children, subsequently transferring wealth for generations to come.

Contents

Introduction

B eing a single mother comes with its own set of challenges, and one of the most important ones is ensuring that your children are taking care of in case something unexpected happens to you. Estate planning is an essential tool that can help you protect your assets, plan your children's future, and provide Peace of Mind. In this book, we will explore the various aspects of estate planning and provide you with a comprehensive guide on how to create a solid estate plan that is tailored to your unique needs as a single mother.

CHAPTER 1

Understanding Estate Planning

This chapter will provide an overview of what estate planning is, why it is important, and the various elements that make up an estate plan. It will also explain the difference between a will and a trust, and the benefits and drawbacks of each.

Estate planning is the process of preparing for the transfer of a person's assets and wealth after their death. It involves creating legal documents and strategies to ensure that your assets are distributed according to your wishes and that your loved ones are taken care of. Here are some of the key elements of estate planning:

1. **Will:** A will is a legal document that outlines how you want your assets to be distributed after your death it also designates an executor to carry out your wishes and may appoint guardians for minor children.

2. **Trusts:** Trusts are legal arrangements that allow you to transfer assets to a trustee who manages and distributes them according to your wishes. There are different types of trust, such as revocable and irrevocable trust, and they can be used for various purposes, such as reducing taxes or protecting assets from creditors.

3. **Powers of attorney:** Powers of attorney are legal documents that designate someone to make decisions on your behalf if you become incapacitated or unable to make decisions for yourself. There are different types of powers of attorney, such as financial and medical powers of attorney.

4. **Beneficiary Designations:** beneficiary designations are used to designate who receives certain assets, such as life insurance policies or retirement accounts, after your death. It's important to keep these designations up to date and coordinate coordinated with your overall estate plan.

5. **Estate Tax Planning:** Estate tax planning involves strategies to minimize the amount of estate taxes that may be owed upon your death. This may include gifting assets, setting up trusts, or taking advantage of exemptions and deductions.

6. **Business Succession Planning:** If you own a business, business succession planning is an important part of estate planning. This involves planning for the transfer of ownership and control of the business upon your death or retirement.

7. **Charitable Giving:** Charitable giving can be an important part of estate planning, both for philanthropic reasons and for potential tax benefits period this may involve setting up charitable trust or including charitable bequests in your will.

Overall, estate planning is a complex and multifaceted process that involves many different elements. It's important to work with a qualified estate planning attorney to create a comprehensive plan that meets your unique needs and goals.

CHAPTER 2

Taking Inventory of your Assets

To create an estate plan, you need to have a clear understanding of what you own and what your assets are worth. This chapter will guide you through the process of taking inventory of your assets, including your home, car, investments, and personal belongings.

An inventory of assets is an important component of estate planning as it helps to ensure that all of your assets are accounted for and properly distributed according to your wishes. Some examples of assets that should be included in inventory or estate planning purposes include:

1. **Real Estate:** This includes any property that you own such as a home, land, vacation property, or rental property.

2. **Personal Property:** This includes any tangible items that you own such as vehicles, jewelry, artwork, collectables, furniture, and household items.

3. **Financial Accounts:** This includes any bank accounts, investment accounts, retirement accounts, and insurance policies that you own.

4. **Business Interest:** This includes any ownership interests that you have in a business, such as stocks, shares, or partnership interest.

5. **Digital Assets:** This includes any online accounts social media accounts, e-mail accounts, and digital media that you own.

6. **Intellectual Property:** This includes any patents, trademarks, copyrights, or other forms of intellectual property that you own.

7. **Life Insurance Policies:** this includes any life insurance policies that you own or are the beneficiary of.

It is important to keep your inventory of assets up to date and to share it with your estate planning attorney or trusted loved ones so that they can properly administer your estate according to your wishes.

CHAPTER 3

Choosing a Guardian
for your Children

As a single mother choosing a guardian for your children is one of the most important decisions you will make. This chapter will provide guidance on how to choose a suitable guardian, factors to consider, and how to have conversations with potential guardians about your wishes.

Choosing a suitable guardian for your children is an important part of estate planning a guardian is someone who will be responsible for taking care of your children if you and your spouse are unable to do so he or some steps to help you choose a suitable guardian.

1. **Identify Potential Guardians:** Consider people you trust, who share similar values and parenting style, and who have the capabilities to take care of your children, you may want to consider family members, close friends, or even a professional guardian.

2. **Evaluate their Suitability:** Evaluate each potential guardian's age, health, financial stability, lifestyle, and availability. Consider their willingness to take on the responsibility of raising your children, and their relationship with your children.

3. **Have a Conversation:** Have an open and honest conversation with your potential guardians about their willingness to serve as your children's guardians. Discuss your expectations, your values, and your children's needs.

4. **Consider Backup Guardians:** Choose alternate guardians in case your first choice is unable to serve or no longer wants to serve as guardians.

5. **Include your Choice in your Estate Plan:** Include your choice of guardians and your will or trust. Be sure to discuss your wishes with your family members and close friends.

6. **Review your Choice Periodically:** As circumstances change, you may need to update your choice of guardians. Review your estate plan periodically and make changes if necessary.

Choosing a suitable guardian for your children is a critical decision and it's important to take the time to evaluate potential guardians and make the best choice for your children's well-being.

CHAPTER 4

Create a Will

A will is a legal document that outlines how your assets should be distributed after your death, this chapter will explain how to create a will, what to include in it, and how to update it as your circumstances change.

Creating a will is an important step in ensuring that your assets and possessions are distributed according to your wishes after your passing here are some steps to follow when creating a will:

1. **Determine What Assets you Have**: Make a list of all the assets you own, including property, investments, bank accounts, and personal possessions.

2. **Decide who you want to inherit your assets:** consider who you want to inherit your assets and how you want them to be divided. You may want to consult a lawyer or financial advisor to help you make these decisions.

3. **Choose an executor:** You may also want to select an alternate executor in case your first choice is unable to fulfill the role.

4. **Draft your will:** you can draft your own will using a will making software or consult with an attorney to create a more comprehensive will that takes into account your individual circumstances.

5. **Sign in date your will:** once your will is complete, sign in dated in the presence of a witnesses who are not named in the will the witnesses should also sign and date the will.

6. **Store your will in a safe place:** keep your original will in a safe and easily accessible location. You may also want to provide copies to your executor and other family members or close friends.

7. **Review and update your will periodically:** review your will periodically to ensure it still reflects your wishes and make updates as necessary.

Remember that creating a will is an important step in estate planning and can help provide Peace of Mind for both you and your loved ones. It is always advisable to seek professional legal advice in creating a will to ensure that your wishes are properly documented and executed.

CHAPTER 5

Setting Up a Trust

A trust is a legal arrangement that can help protect your assets and provide for your children's future, this chapter will explain the different types of trusts available and how to set one up.

There are several different types of trust, each with its own specific purposes and features. Some of the most common types of trust are:

1. **Revocable Trust:** A revocable trust is a trust that can be changed or terminated by the trust creator during their lifetime, these trust are often used to manage assets during the creator's lifetime and to avoid probate after the creator's death.

2. **Irrevocable Trust:** An irrevocable trust is a trust that cannot be changed or terminated once it is created. These trusts are often used for tax planning, asset protection, and charitable giving.

3. **Living Trust:** A living trust is a trust created during the trust creator's lifetime, often used to manage assets during their lifetime and to avoid probate after death.

4. **Testamentary Trust:** A testamentary trust is a trust that is created under a will and becomes effective upon the death of the person creating the will.

5. **Charitable Trust:** A charitable trust is a trust that is created for charitable purposes, such as supporting a particular charity or cause.

6. **Special Needs Trust:** A special needs trust is a trust that is created for the benefit of a person with special needs, to provide for their care and support without disqualifying them from receiving government benefits.

7. **Asset Protection Trust:** An asset protection trust is a trust that is created to protect assets from creditors or lawsuits.

8. **Spin Thrift Trust:** A spin thrift trust is a trust that restricts a beneficiaries assets to the trust's assets, protecting those assets from the beneficiaries creditors.

9. Totten Trust: A Totten trust is a type of revocable trust that is created by depositing money into a bank account in the name of the trust with the beneficiary name as the person who will receive the funds upon the trust creator's death.

It is important to note that the specifics of each type of trust can vary depending on the jurisdiction and the individual circumstances involved it's recommended to consult with a qualified attorney or financial advisor before creating a trust to ensure that it meets your specific needs and objectives.

CHAPTER 6

Minimizing Estate Taxes

E state taxes can be a significant burden on your estate and your heirs. This chapter will explain how estate taxes work how to minimize them, and how to plan for them in your estate plan.

Estate taxes also known as inheritance taxes or death taxes are taxes that are imposed on the transfer of property or assets from a deceased person to their heirs or beneficiaries. The tax is calculated based on the value of the estate and varies depending on the jurisdiction. Here's how estate taxes generally work:

1. **Determine the Value of the Estate:** The value of the estate is determined by adding up the fair market value of all the assets owned by the deceased person at the time of their death.

2. **Calculate the Estate Tax:** Once the value of the estate has been determined, the estate tax is

calculated based on the applicable tax rate, which can vary depending on the jurisdiction.

3. **Pay the Estate Tax:** The estate tax must be paid by the estate before the assets can be distributed to the heirs or beneficiaries.

To minimize estate taxes there are several strategies you can use, including:

1. **Gifting:** One way to reduce the size of your estate and minimize estate taxes is to give away assets while you're still alive, you can gift up to a certain amount per year (currently 15,000 per person) without incurring gift taxes.

2. **Trust:** Trust can be used to transfer assets to your heirs or beneficiaries while minimizing your estate taxes. For example a bypass trust can be used to shelter assets from estate taxes by passing them on to your heirs tax free.

3. **Life Insurance:** Life insurance can be used to provide liquidity to pay estate taxes so your heirs don't have to sell assets to pay the taxes.

4. **Charitable Donations:** Charitable donations can help reduce your estate tax liability by reducing the size of your estate you can donate money or assets to

a qualified charity, and the donation will be deducted from the value of your estate.

It's important to note that the estate tax laws can be complex and vary depending on the jurisdiction. It's a good idea to consult with a financial advisor or state planning attorney to determine the best strategies for minimizing your estate taxes.

CHAPTER 7

Beneficiary Designations and Joint Ownership

This chapter will explain how beneficiary designations and joint ownership can affect your estate plan and how to ensure that your assets are distributed according to your wishes.

Beneficiary designation: Beneficiary designation is a method of transferring ownership of an asset to a named beneficiary upon your death. Typically, this is done by filing out a form provided by the financial institution or insurance company where the asset is held. You can name one or more beneficiaries, and you can also specify what percentage of the assets each beneficiary should receive. When you pass away, the assets will be transferred directly to your named beneficiary without going through the probate process. This means that the assets will not be subject to any claims against your estate, and it will not be used to pay any outstanding debts or taxes.

Joint ownership: Joint ownership is when two or more people own an asset together. There are two types of joint ownership: joint tenancy and tenancy in common. In joint tenancy, each owner has an equal share of the asset, and when one owner passes away, their share automatically transfers to the other owner. In tenancy in common, each owner can have a different share of the asset. And when one passes away, their share is transferred to their heirs according to their will or state law.

Joint ownership can have a significant impact on your estate because it affects the way your assets are distributed when you pass away. If you own an asset in joint tenancy with someone else, the asset will automatically transfer to the other owner when you pass away, regardless of what your will says this means that if you intended for the asset to go to someone else, such as a different family member or charity you would need to take steps to remove the joint ownership designation.

If you own an asset in tenancy in common with someone else, your share of the asset will be included in your estate when you pass away. This means that it will be subject to probate and it could be used to pay any outstanding debt or taxes before it is distributed to your heirs.

It is important to note that beneficiary designations and joint ownership can have complex legal and tax implications, and it's always a good idea to consult with an estate planning attorney or financial advisor before making any changes to your ownership arrangements.

CHAPTER 8

Planning for Incapacity

Planning for incapacity planning for incapacity is an essential part of estate planning. This chapter will explain how to create a durable power of attorney, advanced health care directives, and legal documents that can protect you and your children if you become incapacitated.

A durable power of attorney is a legal document that grants someone else the authority to make decisions on your behalf in case you become incapacitated or unable to make decisions for yourself. Here are the steps to create a durable power of attorney:

1. **Choose an Agent:** The first step is to select someone you trust as your agent, your agent will have the legal authority to make decisions on your behalf, so it's important to choose someone who is responsible, trustworthy, and has your best interests at heart.

2. **Decide on the Scope of Authority:** Determine the scope of authority you want to grant your agent. You

can give your agent broad or specific powers, depending on your needs and preferences.

3. **Draft a document:** You can create a durable power of attorney document yourself, but it's recommended that you seek the help of an attorney. The document must be in writing and include specific language that complies with the laws of your state.

4. **Sign the Document:** you must sign the document in front of a notary public, who will acknowledge your signature. Some states require witnesses as well.

5. **Distribute Copies:** Give copies of the document to your agent, your doctor, your lawyer, and any other relevant parties.

6. **Review and Update:** Review your durable power of attorney periodically and update it as necessary. We need to revoke or amend the document if your circumstances change.

It is important to note that durable power of attorney only takes effect when you become incapacitated. If you become incapacitated and don't have a durable power of attorney, your loved ones may go to court to get a guardianship or conservatorship to make decisions on your behalf.

CHAPTER 9

Reviewing and Updating your Estate Plan

Your estate plan should be reviewed and updated regularly to ensure that it continues to reflect your wishes and circumstances. This chapter will explain when and how to update your estate plan and what to do when doing so.

Estate planning is an essential process that ensures your assets are distributed according to your wishes after your death. However, your circumstances and wishes may change overtime, which means that your state plan should also be updated periodically. Here are some situations that may require you to update your estate planning:

1. **Changes in family circumstances:** Changes in your family, such as births marriages, divorces, or deaths, may require you to update your state plan. For instance, if you get divorced, you may want to remove your former spouse as a beneficiary and your estate plan.

2. **Changes in financial circumstances: Changes** in your financial situation, such as significant increase or decrease in assets, may require you to review and update your state plan accordingly.

3. **Changes in health status:** if you have developed a serious illness or become incapacitated, you may need to update your estate plan to reflect your current health status and ensure that your medical and financial decisions are aligned with your wishes.

4. **Changes in laws and regulations:** changes in laws and regulations regarding estate planning may require you to update your estate plan to ensure that it remains valid and effective.

5. **Changes in personal wishes:** your personal wishes regarding the distribution of your assets may change over time and you may want to update your estate plan to reflect these changes.

To update your state planning, you can either modify your existing document or create new ones altogether. You should also consult with a qualified estate planning attorney to ensure that your updated a state plan is legally valid and effective.

Conclusion

In conclusion estate planning is an essential tool for single mothers who want to protect their assets, plan for their children's future, and ensure Peace of Mind. By following the guidance provided in this book you can create a comprehensive estate plan that reflects your wishes and ensures that your children are taken care of if something unexpected happens to you.